IMAGES OF ENGLAND

NORTHWICH

IMAGES OF ENGLAND

NORTHWICH

J. BRIAN CURZON

The
History
Press

Published as a contribution to Roman Northwich, 2004

First published in 2004 by Tempus Publishing

Reprinted in 2009 by
The History Press
The Mill, Brimscombe Port,
Stroud, Gloucestershire, GL5 2QG
www.thehistorypress.co.uk

British Library Cataloguing in Publication Data.
A catalogue record for this book is available from the British Library.

ISBN 978 0 7524 3149 9

Typesetting and origination by
Tempus Publishing Limited.
Printed in Great Britain.

Contents

The story of Northwich is encompassed in this aerial view of the town. The River Weaver runs from top to bottom with Hunt's Locks in the canalised section and the former winding course of the river to the left, with the sheds of the Boat Club just visible. The impressive viaduct carries the Manchester to Chester railway above the new and old courses of the Weaver and the valley of the Dane. In the centre of the photograph is the junction of the two rivers, with the Roman site on the hill to its left and the medieval centre of the salt industry marked by the gas tower near where the ancient salt pit once was.

Preface

There have been several previous collections of pictures of old Northwich, but this is the first attempt to use pictures to illustrate the story of the town, rather than to present a personal selection or collection to the public. Of course it is impossible to illustrate the entire story, so the images have been grouped to show how the town developed as a major transport centre, and how its main industry of salt making in fact destroyed the old town. Like Jericho of old, the walls of Northwich 'came tumbling down' throughout the nineteenth century. New prosperity was found with the growth of the heavy chemical industry based on salt. Social reform came to the late Victorian town with official policies and generous gifts from the chemical and salt manufacturers. The First World War caused social and economic upheavals, and in the years between the wars, a new Northwich began to emerge, moving away from the sinking centre into attractive garden suburbs.

The former Urban District Council swept away the last crumbling remnants of the old town to replace it with shopping malls and car parks in the 1960s and '70s. All these changes are recorded here. I hope I have presented an interesting selection of images, which may also serve as a directory in which to look up the key facts from the story of the town. It is a fascinating tale of a town which was often at the forefront of local events. It is almost impossible to say where any particular photograph of the interior of salt works was taken. The photographs are given merely as representations of the process, and some may not be in Northwich.

Introduction

The story of Northwich starts in the Triassic period around 250 million years ago. Vast beds of solid rock (rock salt) and hard marl were laid down in alternating desert and shallow sea conditions. They are buried at various depths under mid Cheshire and have provided for its prosperity as the raw material for its salt industry and a vital ingredient in the cheese industry.

Above the Triassic levels are layers of glacial clay, left by the Ice Age. The geography of the town took shape after the ice melted. Low hills which separate Cheshire from Shropshire changed the course of the rivers, so that the Severn, which formerly flowed north, was turned southwards, while the Dane and Weaver were forced to change course dramatically and flow north, meeting in the centre of Northwich. They formed routes for early man from the Mersey to follow the Weaver into Shropshire and the Dane into Staffordshire and beyond. Of early settlement we have few tantalising clues. A few flint flake tools found in the excavations on Castle Hill and a couple of stone axes have been discovered. Only with the Roman occupation can we start to tell the story of the town. Since 1967 excavations have taken place at intervals on Castle Hill, no single fort was revealed on the site but a series of different forts which the Romans called Condate ('the meeting of rivers'). The pattern appears to follow the story which emerges from other northern military sites of a fort in the '70s when the General Agricola (and others) pushed the Northern frontier from the Midlands into Scotland. This was re-occupied at various times and rebuilt with stone defences at the time of military re-organisation under Hadrian, and finally abandoned in the late second century. Northwich's story is made more complicated by the discovery of industrial features. Mid Cheshire has been termed 'the Roman black country' as iron furnaces, pottery kilns and other industrial features provide evidence of a once-flourishing industrial community, perhaps supplying the military to the north. This was also the case with the other Roman towns of the Cheshire plain, when the Romans left the settlement and crossed the river to develop along the Roman road from Chester to York which we now know as North Watling Street. The area we now call Northwich was split into a number of 'townships', most of which were manors in their own right. A manor was land owned by a specific lord, while a township was an area separated from a larger ecclesiastical parish and administered as a separate area. To confuse matters even more, three large parishes met where the rivers join, with Great Budworth, Davenham and Weaverham taking responsibility for various parts. The matter becomes even more confusing as the larger administrative areas, known as 'hundreds', also merged here with Castle in Eddisbury hundred, Northwich, Witton and Leftwich all in the Northwich hundred and the Bucklow hundred extending to the north. The township of Northwich was a small area at the junction of the rivers. In the Domesday Book (1086) no population for Northwich itself is recorded. The earliest maps and records giving details of the town (around 1500) also give the impression that, like Middlewich and Nantwich, it was a salt production area. The salt workers lived in the neighbouring Wych Tune ('town by the wych'). South of the Dane was (and still is) Leftwich, while to the west of the Weaver the area known as Castle included a sparsely populated part of Weaverham parish. Its name probably refers to the Roman fort 'castellum' rather than to an actual castle. No charter for a market or borough is known for Northwich, Middlewich or Nantwich, but all belonged in part to the Saxon kings; as salt-making centres they may have held markets by the ancient right which assumed that markets existing in the time of Edward the Confessor should continue. The salt works had been destroyed in the invasion, but were by then taxed at 35 shillings as trade resumed. Although Northwich remained nominally in royal hands as part of the Earldom of Chester (owned by the Prince of Wales) throughout the Middle Ages it was usually 'farmed out'. That involved a landowner undertaking to pay an annual fee for the right to collect the taxes and rents from the salt maker and keep all profits. In 1484 the manor was given by Richard III to Thomas Stanley in order to buy his support. Stanley famously changed sides at the Battle of Bosworth to bring Henry VII to victory and defeat Richard, for which he was given the title Earl of Derby. Northwich remained the property of the powerful earls until the eighteenth century.

During the sixteenth century, the methods of making salt in the Cheshire salt towns slowly changed. The lead pans that had been used since Roman times for boiling brine to make salt were replaced by ever larger pans made from iron sheets riveted together. The fuel also changed from wood grown especially for the process to coal. Production changed from the small salt houses which were operated seasonally by a largely female labour force, to large factory-size production sheds. The changes which saw the growth of the industrial revolution in the eighteenth century had already taken place in the Cheshire salt industry before what is usually heralded as the 'birth' of the industrial revolution in the cotton industry. The progress of trade and industry was disrupted for a time by the Civil Wars. General Brereton set up a camp where Verdin Park is today and for a time his soldiers based there controlled the Cheshire plain, riding against any resistance. Witton Church still carries the marks made by civil war musket balls on the tower! Northwich also played an important role when Lord Derby, the lord of the manor, was involved in a revolt raised amongst Cheshire men by Sir Robert Booth. They aimed to take Chester and use it as a base to march on London. Instead they marched towards Northwich where they met with the Roundhead army at Hartford and were forced back onto Winnington Bridge. The battle took place in 1659, just a year before Parliament agreed to ask Charles II to return to the throne and was the last time Cavalier and Roundhead met in battle. The development of the salt industry was hindered because nature has provided salt all over central Cheshire, but the coal beds were all around it. How to get the coal to the salt and the salt to the customers was a major problem. Thousands of pack horses took salt away from Cheshire and returned with panniers full of coal. The men were often so involved with the transport that it was the women who were left to boil the brine. In 1670 a search at Marbury for coal for the salt works failed in its original intention. Instead, the first bed of rock salt to be exposed was discovered. Soon mines were opening all over the area and the collapse of the old manorial system with the sale of the manors of Northwich and Witton only hastened the change. No longer restricted by traditional methods and manorial laws, people could buy their own land and develop it for industry and trade almost as they wished. Their uncontrolled exploitation of the salt was to be the ruin of the old town as it sank into its own prosperity.

The story of what occurred is told here in memorable and striking images.

one

Where Rivers Meet

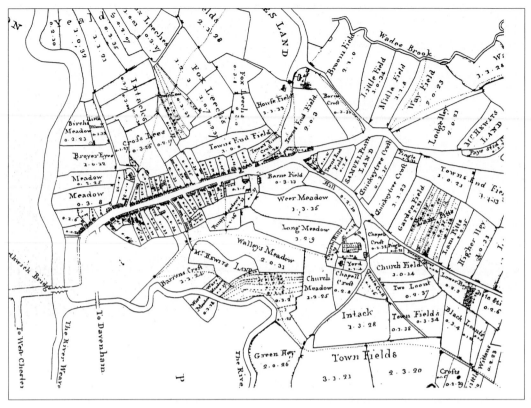

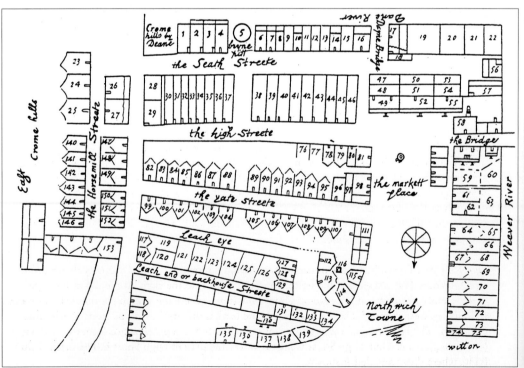

From the air the story of Northwich's past becomes clearer. Most of the photographs which accompany this section date from the 1960s and '70s. Here the Roman road from Chester to York crossed at a ford at the junction of the rivers Weaver and Dane. The line of the road follows the modern roads from the left of this picture and towards the top right corner. Sand banks formed where the two rivers join, making a shallow place for a ford. The ancient Northwich salt-making area is above the river junction. The gas tower marks the approximate site of the medieval salt pit.

Opposite above: In 1721, just as the Weaver Navigation was authorised, the manor of Witton passed from the Vernon family to the Leicesters of Tabley House, and this map was drawn up. The change in ownership hastened the changes taking place in the development of industry. All the houses are arranged along the main Witton Street, the former Roman road. Each stands in their 'burgage plots' where the owner could build a house, grow food and keep small animals. The arrangement of former open fields can be traced in the long parallel fields with the church at a distance from the houses, as was typical in Cheshire.

Opposite below: The earliest known map of Northwich is more of a plan of property than a realistic representation. The Weaver is at the bottom and the Dane is to the right. At the top of the page is 'Crome Hills'; the name still survives as Crum Hill. It was where the 'crumb', or mineral wastes from salt making, were dumped. The circle on the Dane bank is the original salt pit from which brine was drawn. The modern dual carriageway covers the old Seath Street – named from the seathing (simmering) brine, while High Street is shown where the present High Street is. The original Bull Ring, where they were tied, is shown.

Age-old routes met at Northwich, and ancient man used the waterways as part of a cross-country route for prehistoric trade. Using the Mersey, Weaver, Dane and Trent he could cross the country from west to east almost without leaving the water. Via the Weaver he could travel south into the River Severn. Permission was granted to extend the Weaver Navigation into the Dane as far as Middlewich, but it was never completed. Instead, the Trent and Mersey Canal was constructed close to it. The winding course of the Dane Age-old routes met at caused the canal builders to use an easier option. The name Davina (shortened to Dane) is that of a pre-Roman water goddess. The Middlewich to Northwich railway line was built by 1870 to link the salt works of south-east Cheshire to the Cheshire Lines.

The Roman fort site on Castle Hill in 1966 before excavations started, showing the hill-top site with the area first examined in front. The first fort lay between the road and the prominent white house at the centre, defended by steep slopes it was built in the AD70s and reoccupied around AD120. In this area a mixture of military buildings and industrial features have been excavated, suggesting that the hill was used as an industrial area when a second fort was built to its west. The Roman road from Chester to York is marked.

Above: This photograph shows the development of council flats, built over the site at the end of the 1960s. It shows how the fort commanded the crossing of the river which gave it the name of 'Condate'; meaning 'junction of rivers'. A second fort was traced during the 1970s, extending from the bowling green (extreme left) to the chapel in the centre. Finds of flint tools show that early farmers made their homes on the drier uplands overlooking the rivers. The gas tower at the heart of the ancient salt works may indicate where the Romans made salt.

Opposite below: The locks on the Weaver were improved in the 1970s to combat competition in trade from the railways. Leader-Williams, the engineer, built them in pairs with a wide one for sea-going ships and a narrower one for barges, with a narrower sluice to allow river water to continue to flow past. The design assured him appointment as designer of the Manchester Ship Canal.

Right: In 1720 many people who had invested in schemes were ruined when 'the south sea bubble' burst. To control investment the Government allowed investment in specific companies, including the improvement of the River Weaver to allow water traffic to serve local industry. This allowed coal to be brought from south Lancashire and for the export of salt through to Liverpool. The river south of Northwich shows the old winding course and the straight canalised course on the left. The flow is controlled by the sluice gates used to hold back water in dry weather and to release flood water.

The greatest change to the character of Northwich came in 1874 when the partnership of Brunner and Mond built their first chemical works in the grounds of Winnington Hall. The old Hall is near the centre of the picture with the old course of the river frothing over a control weir in front of it. A railway branch line, used to carry limestone from quarries in Derbyshire to the salt supplies from underground by a river link for export, and the delivery of coal, made it the ideal spot for a soda ash works.

Opposite above: At first mines were dug to extract rock salt which was taken to be boiled in tidal water by the Mersey. Later, salty water was pumped from the old mines which eventually collapsed. When the chemical industry was established in Northwich in 1874 those hollows were used to dump waste from the works. From the 1920s this waste was pumped underground into caverns from which brine had been pumped. The old waste lagoons survive as vast white wastelands north of the town and by The Avenue to Weaverham.

Opposite below: A different type of subsidence occurred away from the salt mines. Rain water entered natural fissures in the ground to reach the rock salt beds. It flowed over the top absorbing the salt. Although the salt was pumped several miles away, the ground collapsed where the salt had dissolved from where the water entered. These subsidence holes are sometimes called 'the salt lakes' in a romantic reference to those by the Suez Canal, not the Trent and Mersey!

The railway branch line curves away from the main line to cross the iron bridge, for trains delivering limestone to the chemical works from Derbyshire quarries to the works at Winnington. Northwich moved to the west from the nineteenth century. The area of the former Roman forts was settled again in the

1820s and developed towards the branch line by the end of the century. The long road crossing the picture is Darwin Street, with side streets named after followers of his theory of evolution. Post-war 'garden city' houses and bungalows are seen in the foreground, with larger garden plots.

Above: The town expanded into the rural district in the 1920s with the provision of local authority housing. This was the biggest development in the country under a Government scheme, which allowed businesses to pay local authorities to build rented houses for their workers. Brunner Mond, and later ICI, provided the funding. Rudheath High School can be seen bottom right, the gas tower marks the town centre, while beyond in the distance is the steaming chemical works at Winnington. The Lostock chemical factory is to the right, out of the picture.

Opposite above: In 1938 the Davenham bypass opened to take busy through-traffic between Chester and Manchester away from the town centre. It skirted the estate at Rudheath, which then became an important area in which factories and offices were built, with access to the M6. During the war motor vehicles were stockpiled on one carriageway in preparation for D-Day.

Opposite below: In the early 1970s the town saw great changes with the building of a new shopping centre and 'civic square' which featured the Memorial Hall, Courts, Police Station and County Offices. The old main street had become a pedestrianised area and rear access roads had been provided for delivery to the shops. Underlying this, medieval burgage (house) plots survive along Witton Street. The Witton Albion football ground in the foreground was to be replaced by a hypermarket.

Bypassing the centre was a major achievement throughout the 1960s. Land was purchased and earth was dumped to make an embankment to carry a new bypass past Witton churchyard. The majority of heavy traffic had been taken past Northwich on the Davenham bypass since 1938, but by the '70s the surviving old streets in the town centre were almost traffic-free. Land behind all the properties had been purchased to build delivery roads and provide car parking spaces.

By the end of the 1950s most people had left the centre of Northwich to live in the villages and large estates around the town. Post-war changes in education, and the county policy of segregated education, saw the building of a boy's (front) and a girl's (left) secondary modern school constructed on a campus site at Hartford. The two railway stations and convenient bus routes made it an ideal site for the College of Further Education (top right) as students from all over the county could reach it. Today the playing fields are covered by extensions and mobile classrooms.

two

Crossroads of the Country

From the early seventeenth century, coal replaced wood as a source of fuel, and iron pans replaced lead ones in the salt works. The problem was getting the coal to the salt and the salt to markets. By the early eighteenth century a network of packhorse roads expanded from the Cheshire salt towns into the neighbouring coal fields. Salt was sent on horseback and the same horses returned carrying the coal for the salt works. It was estimated that over 3,000 horses were employed in this trade, which used narrow trails avoided by wheeled vehicles.

During the eighteenth century, Turnpike Trusts undertook to improve and maintain sections of main roads which often followed Roman roads, and charged for their use. This put additional costs onto any goods sent from, or carried into, the towns. At the centre of the county various turnpikes crossed in and near Northwich making it a convenient place to change coaches from cross-country routes. This is the Red Rover coach which passed through Northwich on its way from Liverpool to London and back twice a week until 1837. The men on top are said to be convicts sent for transportation to Australia.

Until 1830 the heavy tax on salt limited the growth of the industry. Almost anyone who was not involved in collecting the salt tax (and Northwich had more tax collectors than any other inland town!) were involved in trying to smuggle the salt past them to the farms and dairies where it was used for making cheese and butter. Many tales are told of the salt smugglers locally. Peckmill, at Bostock, is just one place with links to salt smugglers. It is said that the differing floor levels inside concealed secret hiding places for salt. Women often carried bags of salt out of the works hidden under their wide skirts, and even coffins were used to smuggle the salt out of the town.

Inns at the centre of the town were popular exchange places for the coaches. Stables existed behind most of them for horses to rest and then be used by the next coach to stop. They also provided horses and carriage to rent for local journeys, like modern taxis. With the coming of the railway such services transferred to the hotels near the railway stations, where the stable buildings still stand. The Angel Hotel faced the Bull Ring and provided a selection of rooms, from large private ones at the front, to less expensive ones for servants and poorer travellers at the back and in the attics.

Throughout the eighteenth century, Northwich developed as an inland port. This busy scene shows the old Town Bridge, the court house with its bell to the right and warehouses on the canal side. A special vessel, known as a 'Weaver Flatt', had a flat bottom for easy loading and unloading of salt or coal. The same vessel was used for both – and it was said that they arrived black but left white. Although horses are shown, the usual method of moving the barges was for the crew to pull them along the towpath to Runcorn, and for them to sail over the tidal Mersey into Liverpool.

The old stone Town Bridge was demolished in 1858 as the arches made it difficult for barges to pass it. The new metal bridge was constructed with a headroom of 15ft above the water level, but subsidence was occurring at over 4 inches a year! It soon became necessary for barges to lower their masts when passing and congestion built up again. The timber-fronted towpath was needed to prevent the collapse of the banks because of continual subsidence and flood waters eroding the banks.

The fixed metal bridge was replaced in 1899 by the swing bridge, which is mounted on a floating chamber. The building on the right contained electric winding gear to turn the bridge, using iron wheels which ran on a circular track on a container of air. The weight of the bridge is carried by water, but as no part of it was actually joined to solid earth it was not affected by subsidence. A cantilever effect was obtained by securing numerous cast-iron weights on the short section of the bridge behind the turning platform. Weights could be adjusted to counter the effect of the tilt caused by subsidence.

There was concern that a swing bridge might stick open and prevent any link between the two sides of the town. In order to avoid this, a new road was built to a second bridge. Opened the year before the old bridge was demolished, it allowed road traffic to continue to cross the river while building work was in progress. The Hayhurt Bridge was opened in 1898. The big house above the bridge was home to the surveyors of the Weaver Navigation. Sir Edward Leader Williams improved the locks and conceived the idea of the Anderton Lift. Colonel John Saynor built the swing bridges and converted the Anderton Lift to electricity.

Left: From its start, traffic used the Weaver Navigation seven days a week, but a growing religious revival closed it on Sundays. In order that the men did not waste their Sunday, a church was built on the Roman site with an associated school in 1842. Matching churches were built at Runcorn and Winsford so that no matter where the men were they could attend church and Sunday school. The 1721 Act gave the Trust the right to spend profits on church and road building.

Below: One of the most visible indications of how the town centre has subsided is the Dane Bridge. In Victorian times barges would sail into the Dane underneath the bridge. In 1899 the main girders of the old Town Bridge were sailed under it on barges, to build a new Victoria Bridge for access to the Hayhurst Bridge. Today you could hardly get a raft under it! The black and white bank opened in 1888 at a time when rowing on the rivers was a popular Victorian and Edwardian pastime.

Right: The subsidence in the centre of Northwich has been so dramatic, that in the floods of 1977 the water flowed over the footway of the Dane Bridge. It was raised slightly at the start of the twenty-first century, but it is still almost impossible to believe that anything other than a raft ever passed under it. Flooding where the rivers meet is still possible despite computer controls on the water flow.

Below: Permission to extend the Weaver Navigation into the Dane was obtained in 1724, but, apart from a short length to Baron's Quay (where the magistrates courts stand today), it was never completed. The Dane is the shortest commercial river navigation in the country, as the barges only served the Marshall's salt works on Baron's Quay and this warehouse by the bridge. It was used for transporting raw silk, which was taken by packhorses to the mills of Macclesfield and Congleton. In 1835 a rival Methodist congregation started to meet in this building. By the end of the year it had evolved into the new United Methodist Free Church.

Above: The Crown Hotel was the original meeting place for the Weaver Navigation 'undertakers' and then Trustees. Josiah Wedgwood told a meeting here in 1759 that it had been decided not to bring the Grand Trunk (Trent and Mersey) canal to join the Weaver at Winsford or Northwich as planned because of subsidence risks. Instead it would follow the Dane from Middlewich and then swing around the town. This decision ended any plans to commercially expand plans for a Dane Navigation.

Opposite above: Although the canal bypassed the town, wharves were set up at Rudheath and Wincham where goods to and from the town could be loaded. The Inn at Broken Cross, with stables, warehouses (originally most of the left-hand side of the present pub) and a complex of mills and warehouses at Wincham, testify to a busy trade during the eighteenth and nineteenth centuries.

Opposite below: These stones on the Dane bank near the Memorial Hall are all that is left of an eighteenth-century weir which marked the limit of navigation on the river and the boundary between Northwich and Witton. It was built to control water flow and diverted some of the water to a water wheel in a cotton mill on the Weaver side.

The Grand Trunk Canal skirted Northwich, but its construction caused expansion as industry and trade moved out to its side. Apart from bringing coal into the district from north Staffordshire, in competition with south Lancashire coal on the Weaver, it linked the district to the Midlands and to Manchester (via the Bridgwater) and the various canals radiating from there. Apart from salt and coal, metal goods from the Midlands, pottery from Stoke, beer from Burton and textiles from Manchester went through the area, as did the cocoa beans for Cadbury's in Bourneville.

In 1766 the decision was taken to extend the canal from Anderton to join the Duke of Bridgwater's Canal. This required tunnels at Barnton, Saltersford and Preston Brook. The Duke ordered them to be built wide enough for narrowboats, but they were six inches too narrow for the Weaver flatt boats. The tunnels became major obstacles as they could only be used one way at a time.

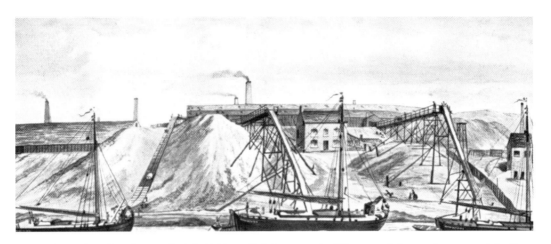

The Duke of Bridgwater had forbidden a link between the Weaver and the canal, as was originally intended, forcing all traffic to use his canal from Preston Brook. A number of 'tips' or slides down which salt could be transferred from canal barges to boats on the Weaver were constructed at Anderton from 1800, where the pub is still nicknamed 'The Tip'. Railway lines (left) were used to move pottery and raw clay.

In 1908 Colonel Saynor, who had built the electric swing bridges in Northwich, converted the lift to be driven by electricity. Cast-iron wheels on the top supported chains with iron weights at the side to counterbalance the tanks of water. It closed in 1984 due to continued corrosion and lack of use. After restoration to reproduce the original hydraulic system, it was re-opened in 2002 to mark the Golden Jubilee of Queen Elizabeth II.

The link between two waterways is best illustrated from above, but best experienced in a boat in the lift.

Navigation Road was built facing the boatyards and offices of the Weaver Navigation. Houses for the workers were built with a raised walkway in front, which was used to make ropes by men walking backwards away from the winding machines, adding new fibre to the ropes. The open field was left in front of the Navigation Offices to provide privacy for the meetings. It is still known as 'The Donkey Field', because donkeys from the boatyards grazed there at night.

This date stone in Navigation Road has a boat's hull carved above. Models like this were used in the boatyards to work out the shape and size of each steel plate used in construction, and several examples from Northwich are preserved in the Boat Museum at Ellesmere Port. One row of houses in Navigation Road had the words 'Temperance Terrace' in blue bricks on the front to show the tenants' abstinence from alcohol. It was painted over thirty years ago!

CEPHAS TERRACE 1859

A view from Highfield over the rooftops of Navigation Road illustrates how they obscure the sheer cliff which protected the Roman fort. Beyond is the junction of rivers and the salt-making area. The clock was once part of a warehouse and was preserved so that bargees could check the time to ensure they arrived in Runcorn when the tide was in.

BOAT BUILDING YARD ON OLD RIVER. NORTHWICH.   Boots 293.

With the development of river transport, Northwich became an important centre for boat building. The yards developed along the river bank and on 'The Old River' away from the main traffic. The boats were built parallel to the river and were launched into it sideways. A whole variety of other industries were linked to the boatyards, including foundries, rope-walks and paint shops.

Beside boats, a host of building repair jobs had to be done to keep traffic flowing on the river. This 1923 scene shows the huge lock gates lifted out by crane for repair, with the church and surveyor's house on the horizon on top of the cliff.

The vessels built by the side of the river could not be launched in the normal way or they would have emerged on the other bank! Huge crowds often assembled to watch a launch, as there was sometimes a massive wave caused by the boat entering the water sideways. Here, one of the ICI steamers is launched into the Weaver.

Many boats built in Northwich are preserved in waterway museums, but they sometimes return 'home' for special occasions. The ICI steamers were all named after local villages. The west bank of the Weaver facing the High Street (seen in the back of this view) is worth a mention as it is technically still 'The Furey Pond'. Furey's salt mine collapsed and filled with water, it was later filled with chemical waste to return it to the original height, and is now a nature reserve!

This boat shed was built so that two narrowboats could be worked on end-to-end at the same time, then launched sideways into the river. It was one of the last boat-building structures to be set up in the town. After the canals went out of use for trading in the 1960s many narrowboats were lined up outside awaiting destruction or conversion into pleasure craft. Today it is still in use for pleasure boat repairs.

Above: At 158ft long the *Athelbrae* was the largest vessel to be built by Yarwoods. It was launched in 1955.

Right: From the 1870s, as competition for trade from the railways grew, most Weaver flatt boats were given steam engines and converted to Weaver packet boats. At the turn of the nineteenth century, processions of them moved up and down the river, each with their little cock boat on top or pulled behind. They were used as a lifeboat or to reach shore from deep anchorage in the Mersey while waiting to use the port at Liverpool.

A group of Weaver packet boats awaiting loading works offers some idea of the volume of trade that was once sent from the district by water.

Part of the ICI fleet at Winnington Wharves. It was the facilities for export by water and to use the river to bring coal from Lancashire which gave the Winnington Works the edge in competition during the Victorian period. After the First World War, lorries provided a more convenient method of nationwide distribution.

Amongst the last vessels to use the river to transport chemicals from Winnington were those from the Scandinavian countries. This one floundered during the 1977 flood and the Weaver's own floating crane came to its aid at the Saltersford Locks.

In 1837 the first major railway from London to Scotland skirted the district, with a viaduct at Vale Royal and a station at Hartford. The platform was built long enough for first class trains to stop, and for a time was important for mail and goods sent to Manchester and Chester by road. Later the convenience of a rail link to London made Hartford a popular residential area.

The Cheshire Lines Railway Company started to build a link from Manchester to Chester, but initially the line split into two on the west of the Weaver with branch lines to Lostock and Middlewich. In 1869 the viaduct was completed carrying the railway over the flood plains of the Weaver and Dane.

The Navigation were keen to protect their trade routes, and neither the Weaver nor the Navigation were to be crossed by solid arches. As with the earlier viaduct at Frodsham, bridges were provided above the waterways so that they could be raised or removed if passage was required on the river. The locks were also made deeper and wider and lined with stone to increase traffic flow.

The Cheshire Lines Company built an impressive station at Northwich to attract customers. There were ample waiting rooms, goods sheds and accommodation for station staff. Passengers were encouraged to travel in comfort, and to improve convenience a covered area linked to the platform was provided where horse-drawn vehicles could collect or deposit travellers.

As the town developed into Leftwich a teacher named Vickers led a campaign to provide a better link to the station for residents, school pupils and students. A footbridge was built over the Dane and the Vickersway route opened under the arches with Vickersway Park by its side.

The first omnibus ran in and around Northwich in 1914, but it proved to be more a novelty than a form of public transport, as many of the journeys were packed with sightseers who had never before been able to visit other villages and towns quite so easily. The development of the service was curtailed by the First World War.

In the years between the wars a busy bus terminus developed putting Northwich at the centre of a network of routes linking most of Cheshire. It was this which was to ensure the continued prosperity of the town centre. The two buses at the traffic lights by St Paul's churchyard are a reminder of the nightly ritual when the inspector's whistle blew at 10.30p.m. for the last buses.

A stately omnibus is seen approaching the Dane Bridge, long before the road became a one-way traffic system and the terminus moved to a new site in 'Watling Street', which was constructed where the row of brick-built shops is shown. When demolished in the '60s, their cellars were found to be flooded!

The Davenham Bypass was opened in 1938 as one of the first of the new roads which copied the German Autobahns and were forerunners of the motorways. This narrow road over Hartford Stone Bridge was replaced by a dual-carriageway. This took the busy traffic between Manchester and Chester away from to narrow streets of Northwich.

Above and below: The old stone bridge at Hartford had caused problems for shipping for some time. In 1938 it was replaced with a modern concrete structure with a steel centre portion which could be raised in case a tall vessel wanted to pass, lifting the roadway ten feet into the air! As war broke out the following year and petrol was rationed, traffic using the new road was reduced, so one carriageway was used to stockpile vehicles awaiting D-Day.

Hunts Lock to the south of town ceased to be of importance for shipping as trade with the river declined from the 1950s. However, it took on a different role as part of a route for residents on the Greenbank Estate to walk over the gates into London Road or to the Grammar School by the river.

Riverdale was developed as playing fields for Sir John Deane's Grammar School in the years between the wars, and it was at this time that a prehistoric stone axe was found there. A rather military-looking vessel is moored by the side in this photograph. Today the houses of the Kingsmead Estate extend along the riverside beyond this point.

The Weaver continued to be a viable water link for the salt and pottery industry during the 1930s when this advertisement was used. During the Second World War plans to extend it as a ship canal joining it to a deepened and widened Trent and Mersey were drawn up, in the hope of a ship canal to Wolverhampton and the Black Country.

Cold weather was always a problem for water transport, as illustrated in this picture at Barnton in 1909. In 1963 the 'big freeze' made every waterway in the country impassable for months. British Waterways ended commercial traffic and many narrowboats were returned to Northwich where they were made and registered to be refitted as pleasure-boats. Traffic had returned to the roads again.

three

Worth its Salt

Following the discovery of rock salt at Marbury in 1670 there was a rush to dig salt mines north of Northwich. They tended to have one or two shafts at the centre and to be dug out in all directions making a circular cavity. They were often dug close to the river for easy export of the rock salt, as shown on this map, but this left them vulnerable to flooding, and today the area north of the town is still unstable. Expensive plans to fill the cavities have yet to be successful.

Visits to mines were popular and visitors were intrigued by the crystals sparkling in the candlelight, and also by the numerous mice which ran everywhere. The rodents were brought down the shafts in the straw and hay for the horses and survived by pinching food from the workmen and horses, or chewing the fatty tallow candles which were the main source of illumination in the mines. A visit to a mine was shown in the *Illustrated London News* in 1850.

One of the things which used to amaze visitors to salt mines then, and can still cause surprise now, is how much room there is. The beds were well over 60ft thick so large chambers could be excavated to extract all the salt. Underground narrow gauge railways carried salt to the shaft while work was often carried on at several levels, cutting away one layer and then another to create high-roofed caverns contrasting with the restricted height of coal mines.

The circular shaft in the roof, the tub with people being hoisted to the surface and the little train of tubs on narrow gauge are all typical of mining. Horses were sent down the shafts as foals but when they became too old to work they were often too big to return to the surface in the tubs – so they were slaughtered underground and sold for dog food. Visitors commented on their shiny coats which were the result of licking the salt.

Over the years it was realised that the thicker the columns which supported the roof the longer the mine would last. Salt mines were too high to use pit props like a coal mine, but owners were reluctant to leave too much salt un-mined. This thick column and the stockpiles of rock salt were photographed around 1900, but it is puny compared to the 60sq.ft of un-mined rock left in the modern mine.

These men, about to be lowered into a mine, are clearly visitors. Their suits, flat caps and polished shoes contrast with the modern-looking jacket of the man in the bowler hat who is presumably in charge of the mine. The circular tubs were used to for transporting both men and the mined rock salt.

Salt mines and works were quick to make use of new innovations. This steam pumping engine was made by the important Birmingham producers Boulton and Watts and installed at Littler's Mine in Marston in 1810. A century later the engine went to the Science Museum in London where it is still the oldest engine on show. The use of steam to pump the brine from 'wild' streams and flooded mines greatly improved the rate of production after the abolition of the salt tax in 1830.

Cast-iron columns which once supported a steam engine are visible in the ruins of the pumping house above Witton Bank salt mine, which has collapsed into a mound of rubble above a pool. A distinguished looking group of men in high hats survey the devastation which was common at the end of the nineteenth century.

By trial and error the best size for a pan was found to be 30ft wide. This allowed huge 'rakes' with handles 15ft long to be used from each side. Different qualities of grain were made by varied boiling times and the addition of traditional ingredients including ox blood, soft soap, and even human urine! In the heat men always worked stripped to the waist and, in an age when bodies were seldom uncovered, they attracted visitors interested in seeing them as much as the process of salt making itself. Victorian photographers provided pictures to record the experience.

For fine table salt the crystals were shovelled into wooden moulds and left to set like huge sand castles. They were taken to the 'hot-house' where the heat passed from the pans under special brick floors to dry the salt. When totally dry it was either sold as a solid block, or taken to be ground into fine table salt and packed in bags or packets. Much salt was used to barter in the West-African slave trade in the early years, and Africa continued to be one of the best markets for bagged salt.

Men would fill a row of tubs which stood on a metal rack hanging from the pan side, and would then fill a second – often on the other side – while they drained. A tap on the side with a wooden 'mundling stick' produced a distinctive note when they were hard enough to be taken to the hot house to bake.

These men were photographed loading common salt. It was piled onto the wooden floor, known as a hurdle, in a heap to drain before being taken to waiting barges or railway wagons on two-wheeled carts and tipped into them. As some of the work involved shifting bags of salt outside, the men wore warm flannel shirts, as well as short 'breeches' to keep the hems out of the corrosive salt. All workers wore clogs.

Victorian moralists campaigned against the conditions in the works where men and women worked together wearing as little as possible. A painting by Philip Holman Miller captures the outrage, showing a woman wearing just a shift, who has stopped to breastfeed her new born baby during her short break from work. She is watched by a semi-naked workman while vagrants sleep in the warm by the stoke hole in exchange for doing a few hours work. The Factory Act of 1870 forbade women and children from working by the pans.

The Salt Union's aim was to buy out every salt works and control the river boats. By concentrating work on a few big works it was able to control prices by illuminating competition. It created problems for workers who were put out of jobs, while those with jobs found their hours increased and their pay controlled. Riots broke out in 1891, with workers protesting against overly long hours for the watermen. These policemen posed outside the police station at the time when extra officers were needed to combat the rioters.

Opposite below: Over the years there were various grouping of works owners who tried to link together to fix prices. However, other works would soon undercut them and the price fixing failed. This cartoon from 1834 illustrates a meeting of one 'association' showing salt manufactures fixing outlandish prices for their salt. In 1888 the slump in trade finally saw most salt works joined together to form the Salt Union.

There was still pride in the salt industry, and arches made with pillars of rock salt covered by block salt direct from the works were set up close to where Timber Lane joins Witton Street during various celebrations at the end of the Victorian era. They resembled the Triumphal arches of ancient Rome. Other arches included one of bicycles, one of chemical barrels and one capped by a fireman and hose.

During the 1988 Heritage Festival it was decided to create a salt arch. However, rock salt was no longer mined in large blocks and the last open salt pans had ceased to function. A construction of lorry pallets was used with plastic bags of salt stacked on them. Apart from the difference in construction it is interesting to compare the state of Witton Street almost ninety years after the previous photograph.

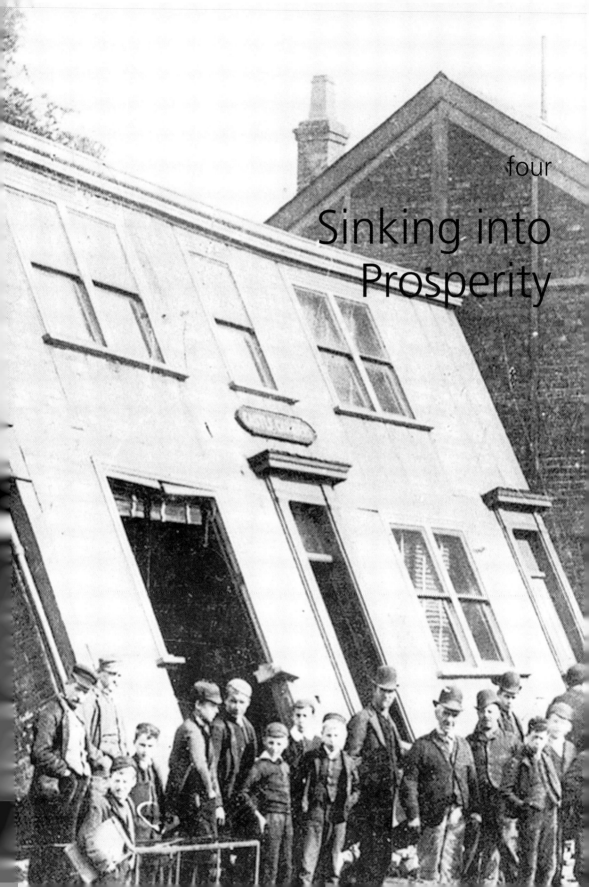

four

Sinking into Prosperity

As the salt was removed from under the town, Northwich itself started to sink into the very source of its prosperity. Throughout the nineteenth century the problems became worse. People would visit the town to see its curious twisted buildings and partly-buried houses. The dangerous living conditions here caused the gradual flow of people from the centre and the decline – of what houses remained – into slums. This scene, close to the present Elizabeth House housing complex, shows how rows of terraced houses sank with the old ground level. Witton Street was raised to keep a level track way leaving the impression that the houses had sunk into a conveniently shaped hole.

One of the major problems experienced as a result of the unstable ground was the preservation of efficient sewers and water supplies. Already damaged buildings became overcrowded and unsanitary as a result, and much of central Northwich became little more than a picturesque ruin. The men who have come to help or just to watch all wear suits and hats – almost all the subsidence photographs from Northwich feature just men.

Opposite below: The roads were raised to their original level around the houses, as the old ground level fell into the spaces left underground by salt extraction. Usually the ground sank slowly by a few inches or even fractions of inches each year, so the houses remained intact but sometimes damaged. Ashes from the works and other waste were tipped onto the road to restore the surface. The old pavement was preserved at the front of these Old Warrington Road houses and a fence was provided to prevent people falling into the hole.

Left and below: Two views of the same building show the philosophical way in which people considered subsidence as an occurence that, if it happened, was something you had to put up with. The first photograph shows the back wall of a house in Leicester Street which has fallen down. The second view shows the same house after it has totally collapsed. Two young couples and their child pose on the ruins of their former house to be recorded on a postcard!

Twisted walls, cracked brickwork and shattered windows are the results of property collapsing into its foundations. The remnants of iron railings and the arched doorways show that this was once good-quality housing. What appears to be flapping curtains from broken windows on the right is actually a woman in a long apron sitting in a window with a child in a 'pinnie' standing on the ledge next to her. As two young men sit in the next window, is it possible they were still living in such conditions? The entry is the way into Arnold's Court, a group of houses arranged around a yard behind.

Practically the whole of the old town centre slowly sank, and damage caused by subsidence – like these twisted windows and door – resulted in the need for housing to develop further and further away from the town centre. Yet at the same time visitors flocked to see the damage and purchased postcards like this one of the misery in the town. This is probably in London Road.

While the buildings subsided, life and trade continued, almost as if nothing had happened. To allow for the subsidence Northwich became a town of steps. They led down into sunken shops while others were reached up flights of steps. The regular floods made shops like this even harder to maintain.

Right: It was realised that a timber framework held bricks together better than any other building method. Linked with the Victorian aesthetic movement and the vernacular revival of Tudor house types, it created a picturesque look for the town centre. This fanciful building in High Street was a bank with a brick and stone ground floor. It was damaged by the subsidence, but an ornate upper floor remained intact on props while a new timber-framed ground floor was built.

Below right: As it became usual to live out of town and have lock-up shops in the town, fewer ornate timber-framed structures (little more than sheds with windows at one end) were built. There was no need for residential areas upstairs, they were also lighter to 'lift' and cheaper to replace – as many have been today. They are a speciality building of the salt district.

Opposite below: The collapsed wall of a house in the town shows the bedroom floor – as the downstairs rooms have already sunk below the ground level at which the men are standing. To the right, flowered bedroom wallpaper and the line of a roof with a chimney stack shows that the house next door had already sunk by another storey beneath that. As the entire centre of the town sank into the collapsing salt beds the need for better housing became ever more urgent. This was provided on more stable land outside the town.

Left: When a terraced house collapsed, damaging the buildings beside it, it was realised that leaving a small space between buildings allowed each one to move separately, as is illustrated here next to the Dane Bridge where two buildings lean at different angles. All the shops in the shopping centre are separated from the ones next to them for this reason.

Below: This building near the Bull Ring was raised using hydraulic jacks to lift the wooden 'raft' on which it was built. Alternating timbers were laid at the corners to carry the weight while new courses of brickwork to support the structure at its new level were laid. Northwich uniquely developed a special style of its own to combat the industrial exploitation of its geology, and was a place where 'shoplifters' were welcome!

Opposite below: Probably the best known image of Northwich subsidence, when Castle Chambers collapsed backwards. Even the glass in the windows remained intact! It show how the provision of space between structures allowed them to move independently. The angle at which it came to rest is made more dramatic in this photograph when compared with the men standing in front.

Above: While steps would lead down to some buildings they also lead up to property which had 'come up in the world'. In order that 'lifting' was not needed too often they were usually raised well above the road level and steps were provided to the door. Northwich is still a town of steps. The heavy timber 'raft' on which the frames were set is clearly seen in this picture and the temporary wooden steps would have been replaced by more substantial ones when the foundations were complete.

If all else failed, Northwich's half-timbered building could be put onto rollers and moved! The Bridge Inn stood next to the Dane Bridge in London Road. In 1891 the top part was put onto rollers and moved to a new site away from the river. After the 1946 floods it was decided to raise it above flood level, which was recorded in this photograph from 1953. It is worth standing by the steps to appreciate just how deep that flood was.

This dramatic view from the Dane Bridge into London Road is in stark contrast with the street today. Pools of water cover the road and buildings are toppling over. Wooden hoardings for posters show where other buildings have been destroyed by previous collapses. Even today the buildings which line this road have their doors above the 1946 flood level and are reached by steps or ramps.

Looking across London Road above the pools of water left by subsidence and flood. The industrial building in the foreground is typical of many in old Northwich that were constricted like sheds from planks to be light-weight, easy to demolish and rebuild on another site in case of collapses. Notice how unconcerned the man sitting on the foundations of the building opposite is by the devastation.

This row of terraces close to the railway arches in London Road show all the problems of the old town; windows twisted out of shape, one on the right has been replaced with a new lintel, and roofs are sagging and leaking. The dresses of the girls outside indicate this was taken in the 1920s.

Post-war construction on the same site shows how the houses were arranged in pairs, and how each pair has an exposed steel foundation raft for future lifting. They were built with a steel framework to provide support in the event of further subsidence – however the ending of 'wild brine' pumping and its replacement with a method of filling the cavities with chemical waste has ended the disasters recorded here. Some slow movement does, however, continue.

Even those areas which escaped the worst effects of subsidence slowly decayed until they were uninhabitable. The Bleeding Wolf on the corner of Market Street stands next to the wooden Market Hall; both of them survived into the 1960s. The condition of the cobblestones shows that this area had yet to be troubled by too much sinking in 1891.

Also in Market Street, a watchmaker and jeweller provided a clock on the wall. Personal watches were becoming more common in Victorian times but public clocks were needed in an era before time checks on radio so that workers were not forced to work extra unpaid time. Factories had to record when and on what public clock their own clocks were set weekly.

The narrow winding roads from the medieval period survived, and as can be seen a horse and cart could only just pass the Red Bull and properties in the cobbled Applemarket Street next to the present market. The narrow road, only wide enough for a two-wheeled trap cart, is still used for access to the market car park.

Interesting aspects of a past townscape emerge from old photographs; this street has natural glacial boulders set at intervals to deflect the passing iron-bound cartwheels. The further pub sign has the trademark of Sandiford's Brewery; a cross section of a salt mine shaft.

Above: In 1891 The Brine Subsidence Compensation Board hired the Warrington photographer Birtles to record all the property in the area likely to subside. To take this picture the photographer had simply moved from the pub next door, to the one opposite, the Seven Stars, to take another view, arousing the curiosity of workmen in the warehouse next door.

Right: Only a fraction of the old pubs survive today, and all have been rebuilt since the days of subsidence. Many ceased to be viable as pubs, as the customers moved out of town and television reduced the need to go out in the evenings. The Red Lion at the end of Crown Street now houses a travel agent.

Opposite below: Pubs and shops in a cobbled street might appear picturesque today but the metal plaques on the front of the Fox Inn in Applemarket Street show it is collapsing. These properties were where the modern market car park was built in the 1960s.

The front part of the Wheat Sheaf was replaced with a single-storey building, and was demolished in recent years as part of the redevelopment of the area. The advertisement for stabling recalls the story of a horse and cart which were said to have vanished into a subsidence hole here!

The Sportsman's customers moved away. Timber–framed and plank–lined walls made the upstairs unsafe for hotel guests, while damp and lack of repair took its toll. Once left empty, vandals did the rest. Fire has destroyed many of the town's best timbered buildings.

This photograph was taken where the modern Crum Hill car park is now. The Penrhyn Arms was named after Lord Penrhyn, the eighteenth-century owner of Winnington Hall. It survived into the 1960s when it was a favourite meeting place for people using the Memorial Hall.

Crum Hill kept the name of the ancient rubbish dumps recorded on the sixteenth-century map. It was close to where the service area off Crown Street is now, and was at one time notorious for 'doss houses' where the homeless would sleep on the floor. The name was reused in the 1960s for a different site – as were several old names like Sheath Street and Witton Street.

Left: Cholera came to Northwich in the 1830s, having travelled on ships to Liverpool from India, and was then carried down the river. The germs spread because of poor sanitation and shared privies. The subsidence continually destroyed sewage and fresh water pipes and new ones were continually laid as the streets collapsed.

Below: Smart new fronts were often added to damaged buildings. On the left of this block was Hall's book shop, the publisher of many postcards of old Northwich. The road is ravaged by subsidence and covered with a thick layer of horse droppings.

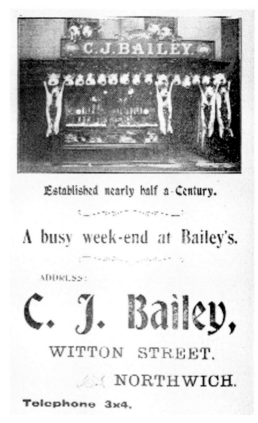

Despite the horse droppings and other pollution, Victorian shopkeepers continued to display their food and wares in conditions which would horrify the public health inspectors of today. This picture has been created for effect in an advertisement, but animal carcasses hanging outside butchers were the norm.

A 'Fent' is a remnant of fabric. Before the First World War, ready-made clothes were hardly known and women purchased remnants to make clothes and household goods. This shop in High Street would sell remnants from the Lancashire mills for home dressmakers.

The men in their showy white fustian trousers lean on a fence outside a little shop window in a row of terraced houses in Leicester Street. Victorian housewives shopped for essentials from little front-room shops in small daily quantities, budgeting from day to day.

Castle Street at the start of the twentieth century showing the Sportsman's Hotel on the left. Beyond the spire of Waterman's church there was never any subsidence, as higher land involved more digging to reach the salt. Note the entrance steps to the solicitors on the corner, now entered at ground level.

The Bull Ring is pictured after 1929 when the Building Society was built. Over the entrance a 'flapper' is shown carved in the year of the 'flapper election' when women voted for the first time. The road is still cobbled and practically traffic-free.

All the ills and ailments of the old buildings are captured in this photograph of Witton Street in February 1892 for the Compensation Board Records: filthy streets with horse droppings churned by the passing traffic, buildings collapsing into their foundations with narrow alleyways and a warren of out-outbuildings behind.

The photographer returned in July to take pictures of the buildings on Witton Street in 1892 with its old library and brick buildings. Fires in the timber buildings, as well as the need for change, later contributed to the vanishing of the old town and its replacement with twentieth-century buildings.

The move into Hartford started with the Marshall's, who moved into Hartford Hall and other houses away from their town centre works during the Regency period. The station, with its direct route to London, made it popular in the Victorian period with followers of the Cheshire Hunt, and managers who found it convenient for Winnington Works but far enough away from the pollution.

five

Tides of Change

This Edwardian view shows that London Road beyond the railway viaduct was hardly damaged by subsidence. The workhouse was shielded from view behind polite trees on the right. The Victorian Poor Law joined a number of parishes into Poor Law Unions with their own central workhouse. This was the first step towards modern local authority control as Northwich became the centre of a Union responsible for other matters than just the poor.

The Local Board of Health was part of a national provision for improving conditions from 1874. The boards of responsible people would provide good water supply and sewers, supervise building construction and help create a better living environment financed by the rates. This would improve standards of living and public health as a result. This photograph shows (by their name on the window) that they used rooms at the Talbot: one of the more substantial hotels in the town near the Timber Lane junction with Witton Street.

Meeting of The Town Council of Northwich
What! A Site (sight)

The Urban District Council governed the town from 1884 until Local Government Reform in 1974, and oversaw the reformation of the area from a warren of back streets and ruinous buildings into the town we see today. It took traffic away from the old main streets and developed new housing estates on the outskirts, away from the risk of subsidence. This fun postcard shows one of their meetings, which were held in the Council House, formerly Witton Grammar School, in Church Road.

Witton churchyard was overcrowded with graves and was already full by Victorian times. Burial rights were taken over by the Local Board who purchased land next to the old burial ground to lay out a large cemetery area and two linked chapels; one was equipped for the Catholic requiem Mass and the other for nonconformist services – previously non Anglicans held outdoor burial services. This was an important aspect of health control in the nineteenth century as careful disposal of the dead prevented the spread of disease.

The first thing the Local Board did was to buy up the manor rights, including the market rights. They commissioned Douglas of Sandiway to prepare this drawing for them. It provided more sanitary conditions in which goods, particularly food, could be sold and a cleaner environment in which to shop.

The Market Hall remained in use until its replacement in the mid-1960s. It was also used for dances and other functions, but on a site surrounded by the narrow old streets shown here it was hardly convenient in an age of motor traffic. Besides its use for selling goods it was often used for meetings and even dances.

As the town developed further into Leftwich, away from the subsidence, the problem of moving sewage from that part of town to treatment works north of the town was realised. This little building by the arches was provided to pump it past the subsidence areas, thus avoiding contaminating the river as it entered the town.

The Verdin family were known as 'Kings of Salt'. They made a fortune from salt making and transporting it on the river. They were also major shareholders in the Salt Union. William Henry Verdin was a great benefactor to the district in the last two decades of the nineteenth century, but with the dawn of the twentieth century he moved to a Herefordshire castle.

Robert Verdin, Henry's brother, was MP for Northwich until his death in 1887, after only little more than a year in office. He is remembered by a statue in the park which was opened in his memory and to mark the Golden Jubilee of Queen Victoria. The park offered a breath of fresh air, while the baths were used for exercise and cleanliness in the 'slipper baths'; both an important contribution to public health.

Unfortunately the land chosen for the baths was unstable and collapsed. However at the time there were hopes of developing the town into an inland spa with bathing facilities and the chance for exercise in the park. The relief of athletic youths is above the changing room while the main swimming bath was constructed like a huge salt pan from iron sheets.

Many things which we now expect to be provided by the State were subject to charity provision and local subscriptions in Victorian times. Winnington Bank House was presented by Robert Verdin to become the Victoria Infirmary. The old house is now used for administration, and the timber-framed wards used for convalescing patients who are supervised from Leighton Hospital near Crewe.

In 1897 amidst pomp and ceremony the Verdin Technical School was opened to mark the Golden Jubilee and to provide the equivalent of secondary education today in science, technical studies, arts and crafts, and office skills for an expanding workforce who mainly attended evening classes. It was built well away from subsidence risk, from academic red bricks.

In 1874 John Brunner (left) and Ludwig Mond started the chemical business at Winnington, which processes local salt from brine along with limestone imported from Derbyshire. This makes soda ash, a valuable chemical which is used in a host of industries from glass-making to soap. Brunner was the town's MP and was responsible for many improvements in Northwich. Both men lived at Winnington Hall for a time. As Mond's wife did not approve of Brunner's marriage to his house-keeper they seldom met socially in public but remained personal friends.

Opposite above: The interior of the Technical School is rich with stained-glass windows, including the Verdin coat of arms. At the bottom Robert and William Verdin are pictured with the great scientists of the Victorian period in a conspicuous lack of humility. It remains part of the College of Further Education, and is currently used for art classes.

Opposite below: The Brockhurst at Leftwich was William Henry Verdin's residence, where he entertained the Prince of Wales (later Edward VII) in the late nineteenth century. He purchased Darnhall Hall near Winsford before moving to Herefordshire. It served as a nightclub in the 1960s but is now used as apartments.

Having lost the election to Robert Verdin, Brunner left Winnington in the care of managers and set off on a world-wide cruise. When he returned in 1887 his adoring workforce took the horses from his carriage to pull him home to Winnington. This contrasts to descriptions of the workers as the 'white slaves of Winnington'. Most workers could see no point in joining a union, but early trade unionists even sent 'flying pickets' to the works until they did.

Opposite above: This workman is loading bags of chemicals in the works at Winnington without any protective clothing at all. Although the filling is automatic the presence of a shovel shows that spillages were expected. Although there were good, well-paid jobs at Winnington there were less popular ones involving hard work and dirt until post-war years. Many Irish families came to the town prepared to do them, and, after the war, language problems meant they were the only jobs that some Polish refugees could do.

Opposite below: Working conditions at Winnington were often appalling by today's standards. These two photographs from the Winnington archive show nineteenth-century attempts at protective clothing on trial there. Men often returned home covered in white soda ash – one reason for the term 'white slaves' but shunned the company bath house preferring the comfort of a tin bath on the hearth.

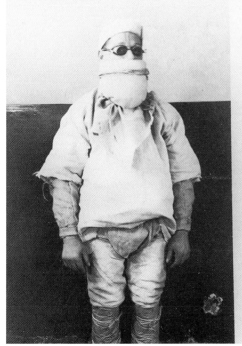

Brunner was keen that Northwich had a Local School Board. This was an optional provision up to 1902. Many rural areas were content to let churches provide any schools in the area. As a Unitarian with a Jewish partner Brunner did not want a workforce dominated by people educated in the Anglican Church. School Board provision ensured pupils received a non-denominational religious education. This picture is actually at Barnton, but in Victorian schools, boys were trained for the factory floor while girls learned to be wives and mothers.

WINNINGTON PARK SCHOOL,
NORTHWICH.

Certificate of Merit

AWARDED TO

William Shaughnessy

FOR

Perfect Attendance
One Year.

Signed

John W Button. Teacher

H. W. BOWKER, A.C.P., A.R.S.I.
Headmaster

Date Easter 1925

Winnington School was well respected despite its strong links with the company, with whom most pupils could expect a job. Considering the position of the school in the works the image chosen hardly seems appropriate for a perfect attendance certificate issued in 1925 – it seems more appropriate to truancy in an the countryside!

Opposite below: Winnington has long links with education. In the 1850s Miss Bell ran a school in the hall for young ladies, seen here on the lawns. It was visited by George Halle of the Orchestra and Professor John Ruskin the art critic. Brunner provided the fist public library in a village there and it had the last company-owned school in the country until the 1870s.

Mond's generosity locally was usually less conspicuous, but in the Long Gallery at Winnington he started to collect paintings, at first just for decoration. It developed into one of the world's great private collections of Renaissance work. On his death it was left to the National Gallery and is now the basis for displays in the Sainsbury Wing there.

The Library Act of 1850 allowed local authorities to finance libraries as long as two-thirds of the electors voted in favour. Brunner demolished three shops to build a library in 1885. The central entrance had rooms on either side which were rented as offices to pay the library bills. A librarian's flat upstairs allowed a lower than usual salary to be offered. This replacement building opened in 1909 on the site; and still contains former offices and flat – now used for administration.

six

Emerging from the Ruins

The new century had hardly started when Britain went to war with Germany in 1914. Most local men were involved in the fighting, while Brunner Mond increased their production of ammunition, employing hundreds of women munitions workers. This was the first time that women had been able to undertake jobs previously only considered appropriate for men, and was the start of women's entry to the workforce.

While work was mainly undertaken by women, they were still supervised by a handful of men. All wore identical uniforms, with the first trousers worn locally – for modesty. Individual collars and bows on the hats allowed for individuality while military style stripes are on the arms of three women. This major change in the way of life locally – and a major contribution to the war effort by local women – only warrants a single sentence in the official company history!

Witton Street was decorated for the return of men from the front in 1918. The Japanese flag was appropriate as they were Britain's ally in the First World War. The war was a great turning point. Many men were killed or too injured to work and women were to continue in many jobs, especially as there was an imbalance in the numbers of young women and men, and many women remained unmarried or young widows.

Until 1909 and Lloyd George's 'People's Budget', provision for those unable to earn a living had been provided through the workhouse. Then a 'dole' payment was made and Labour Exchanges were introduced. Here soldiers with walking sticks and men with bikes (to ride to any job opportunities they may be offered?) are amongst those pictured outside the Labour Exchange; the women are probably going to use the post office next door.

Many men returned from the forces with horrific injuries. Local houses were converted to serve as emergency hospitals. The Ley was one such example in Winnington. The medical and nursing service at such homes, as with hospitals, were all provided out of charity funds. The National Health Service only took over local hospital provision after 1947.

As the works opened in Winnington Park there were no homes and few facilities for the workers near to it. An estate village developed with open spaces, playing fields and a variety of housing in an area still called Winnington Park. Life was pleasant, and there were no pubs to lead the workers into 'bad habits'. Souvenir postcards were sold to visitors.

From 1907 Brunner Mond provided emergency housing for their workers in four-roomed prefabricated bungalows along The Avenue, near the works. Until the 1950s influxes of new workers were provided with temporary homes by the company and then re-housed by the local authority. Many Polish refugees lived in ex-military barracks and worked for ICI after the Second World War, before taking up residence locally.

From 1921 a new estate developed at Rudheath for employees at the Lostock works. The garden city-style houses were provided by the local council with financial help from the company. It was to become the biggest estate financed in this way in the country, and still retains its attractive gardens and homes far superior to most in the old town.

In 1923 Brunner Mond celebrated its Golden Jubilee with a fair for the workers, who were provided with free fairground rides and refreshments. After much deliberation it was decided that men who wanted one would get a free glass of beer, although only soft drinks were offered for women. Old horse-drawn showman's caravans and lorries used to transport the rides behind steam traction engines are featured here.

Crowds of workers and their families were invited to enjoy a host of rides and everyone dressed for the part. There were decorative arches at the entrance to the field and addresses by the managers. Afterwards managers and their guests retired for a more elite celebration dinner at the Hall, which had become a private club to which only the most senior managers were admitted.

An elderly couple, old enough to remember when the works were founded, take their rest on the steps to one of the rides, perhaps remembering days gone by in Winnington Works.

Change came in 1926. The country was hit by the depression and the General Strike, Brunner Mond entered into a merger with three other chemical firms to create the Imperial Chemicals Industry (ICI) to take over trade in their products within the empire. Here the first board of directors is pictured, at the centre with the moustache is Sir Alfred Mond (later Lord Melchet) who became the leading figure in the new company. His Parliamentary work was instrumental in the founding of the Jewish state in Palestine.

Many opportunities opened up for working women between the wars. Amongst them was Broadhurst's 'bakery in a garden' on the old munitions work site at Gadbrook.

Total segregation with women on the tables at the front and men behind was the order of the day in the works canteen, and most women arrived on bikes from the nearby Rudheath estate operating machines to make cakes, pies and biscuits which the men delivered.

The Pavilion Theatre where the Regal car park is now, provided live entertainment in the town before being used to show the first silent movies. It was demolished after damage in the 1946 flood, as it could not compete with the two modern cinemas in the town whose auditoriums were designed for the 'talkies' and demonstrated new developments in projection. One of them is now a bingo hall.

Opposite above: Close to Broadhursts, Roberts opened their bakery which boomed with the introduction of sliced bread made using mass-production methods. It still distributes its products over a large part of the region from a base by the Davenham Bypass at Rudheath. The easy road link to the M6 has seen that area develop considerably in recent years as regional and national business centres. This has totally changed the character of the workforce yet again.

Opposite below: The need for steel to reinforce buildings in Northwich was one reason why Park's Steel Works was set up at Lostock. The vast storage sheds for stockpiles are pictured here. Changes in industry in the later part of the twentieth century saw the works replaced by an 'out of town' shopping development on the site. The iron industry in the area has a long history going back to the Roman site on Castle Hill where there were blacksmith's hearths while foundries for making salt pans flourished in the nineteenth century.

The State Theatre was in the course of construction when the Second World War broke out. Like the cinemas in the town it was built with a steel reinforced concrete frame and brick infill at the front, but the auditorium and stage areas were hung with lightweight cladding. Work never resumed with the peace and it was eventually demolished in the 1970s and replaced by a Job Centre. The fish shop is typical of the single-storey shops which were once a feature of this part of the town.

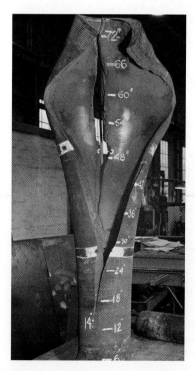

Developments in chemicals and explosives were made locally during the First World War, and as war broke out again in 1939 ICI had just launched commercial polythene production. It was to be a vital ingredient in early radar as an anti-static insulator. After the war it was to become a household name but problems with explosions and burst pipes like this were common. Loud bangs when the polythene plant roof was blown off were not uncommon!

Early experiments with the jet engine at Trafford Park were hit by bombing. The trials moved to a salt works at Marston where it was perfected. Although work was done under top secret conditions the noise caused many rumours about what was being done behind closed doors. Early experiments in the development of a British atom bomb were carried out at Winnington as so many scientists in a chemical works would not arouse enemy suspicion.

The old Waterman's Arms and a shop were demolished to make way for the present half-timbered building. During the war it was much frequented by American servicemen and their girlfriends, who always called the landlady 'Mar Kenyon' as she would cook the food which they supplied for them and was not on ration – sharing it with other customers. Northwich people were fond of 'going to Mar's'! It is now renamed the Witton Chimes.

In 1946 a flood was created by a combination of bad weather, high tide and inadequate river control. London Road south of the crossroads looks like a cross between Venice and Dodge city with its row of single-storey shops looking very like those in a wild west town! The State Theatre is seen between the shops and the gas tower.

The slight bank to the Hayhurst Bridge has allowed the photographer a dry space to stand while picturing the flood. The houses in Jubilee Street had sunk so low that their downstairs windows were at road level. They remained in use until the end of the 1960s despite continual flooding, and were jokingly known as 'the houses where the tide came in'.

Water flowed right over the Town Bridge in the flood, and the bridge was hit by a barge which had broken loose from its moorings. 'The Happy New Era' sign was an advertisement for electrical goods which were just becoming available again after the war. The King and Queen were due to visit the town only a few months after the water fell and all effort was put into cleaning away the mud from the streets for them to drive through.

There was even a boat in Castle Street after the flood. They were used to deliver goods to people on the top floors or to rescue them and take them to safety. The buildings on the right were all cleared recently and replaced with a twenty-first century housing development by the river – it is built on high foundations in case of flood.

Fire is an ever-present problem for timber-framed buildings, and was one reason why people left the town centre to move into more traditional brick homes on the outskirts. Fire, sometimes in suspicious circumstances, has robbed the town of several attractive and important timber-framed buildings since the war and their replacements have not always been as attractive.

Neglect and lack of sympathetic care have ensured that other buildings were lost. The old White Lion had been too altered over the years to be safe. Despite hopes for it to be preserved, an unsympathetic inspector and a brewery which wanted to get rid of it sealed its fate. A decade later and the site still awaits redevelopment, and the pleasing façade has been replaced by a wooden fence.

Change came to an unexpecting group of residents in 1969. The traditional winter parking place for many fairground workers was by Old Warrington Road in Northwich. The 'fairground' site stood in the way of the Albion Way access road. They were given another site in Saxon's Lane, but it flooded regularly and they moved to a site in Winsford ending an ancient link with the town.

James Dean of the Northwich fairground was instrumental in founding the Showmen's Guild (their union and trade organisation) and served as its secretary. Many fairground family graves were dug around his monument in Witton churchyard. The fairground was open during the war years – except during a risk of an air raid – and was popular with American service-men as a place to meet girls.

The Memorial Hall was opened in 1962 as the result of collections and fund raising locally. During the war the lack of reasonable social facilities had been acutely felt. A multi-purpose hall was built to serve as a living war memorial. In the early years the hall was the venue for teenage dances at which chart-topping groups and performers were booked to provide music for dancing. Amongst them were The Beatles who performed four times in the hall.

In 1974 a riot on the field occurred when The Beatles appeared to crown the Carnival Queen. The fans swarmed forward to see the band, who fled in an old van. The Queen was eventually crowned in a more secure environment, on stage in the hall that evening, while outside screaming fans who had been unable to get into the hall watched through the windows. The day was hit by heavy rain and the pandemonium caused the coining of the word 'Beatlemania'.

Above and below: The area outside the Memorial Hall was planned as the Town Square for recreational purposes. Today it is a venue for teenagers to congregate and ride skateboards. Only once did it revert to the medieval use of a town square when, in 1973, the students from the Mid Cheshire College put their Rag Queen, Rag Prince and committee chiefs in the stocks. A charge was intended for throwing rubbish from the market at them, to boost profits to the Charity funds in 1973. However, the expected crowds, afraid of becoming targets themselves, kept away and it was left to friends and fellow students to do the throwing.

The waterways through the town tended to be ignored throughout much of the late twentieth century. Occasionally life returned with the annual Regatta on Whit Monday, or as is shown here when students from Hartford College congregated on the Dane in 1964 for the tug of war over the water. The old Police Station can be seen in the background.

The main difference with this team pictured ten years later is that the men's hair is much longer. Attractive walkways have replaced the old police station and a new one is across the road. A magistrates court now occupies the site but spectators keep a safe distance from the waters edge. On one notable Dane tug of war both teams turned up but no one had remembered to bring a rope!

Also in the 1960s, 18-Plus members from the region converged on the Weaver for their annual raft race. The 18-Plus group provided a social outlet for people between the ages of eighteen and thirty as does its successor Northwich Plus Group.

Members of 18-Plus certainly enjoyed getting wet and muddy. Here the group are pictured after another watery afternoon helping clear the Trent and Mersey Canal. Voluntary work was an important aspect of their social calendar.

Traffic is only now returning to the Weaver after a long spell when it was not accessible to pleasure boats as the Anderton Lift was closed. Since this picture was taken as a postcard in the 1960s the overgrown towpath has been made into a pleasant paved riverside walk. The two baskets on the pole were used to signal between the tow bridges so that one did not open until the other had closed to prevent both sticking open at the same time.

Flower Power came to Northwich in the Rag of 1967 with this float presented by design students It is pictured before setting off from Hartford College in a parade which was headed by Miss United Kingdom, Jennifer Lowe, a former Northwich Grammar School pupil. Also in the parade was Miss Nantwich, later to become Miss England, Miss UK and Miss Great Britain.

Twenty years after that Rag Parade, the author suggested that the Battle of Winnington Bridge (the last combat between Royalist and Cavalier in 1659) be re-enacted at the Moss Farm sports fields which had been given to the town by ICI. It was held again, but administrative problems took it to Oulton Park race course where it was held eleven years too early for an anniversary and many miles from the original site!

Northwich Victoria were founders of the 2nd Division, but left after losing every away game they played. In 1984 they were more victorious and actually went to a Wembley final. It was the FA Trophy, rather than the FA Cup that they won in a replay at Stoke-on-Trent that year.

Castle was the last area to be cleared under the slum clearance programme. The smallest house in town (next to the chip shop) was one victim. Squeezed between two existing buildings, it had needed only a front and back wall and a roof, so was built at low cost in an age without controls around 1830. It was condemned as unfit for modern living.

Development of the Castle area from the 1960s allowed investigation of small parts of the two Roman forts of Condate. Although limited and always in advance of redevelopment they showed signs of metal working hearths, pottery kilns as well as the barracks and defences of the timber forts. The early nineteenth century housing of Castle developed as it was a desirable place to live away from subsidence, smoke, fires and floods.

Throughout the excavations areas of cobble stones like the one being excavated here were discovered showing that around AD 100 the area had been important for iron working. The furnaces were used to soften old iron so that it could be re-worked by blacksmiths and it seems to have been a military supply base for soldiers fighting further north.

The prize find was an iron helmet, uncovered in a pit with parts of two others. After cleaning, its decorative form, typical of auxiliary's helmets, was discovered and a reconstruction was commissioned by the Salt Museum.

It was an exhibition of finds from the first excavation in 1967, at which the surviving remnants of the old Salt Museum were displayed, that caused the move to re-found the museum which was put into store when the building was needed by the Social Services during the war. The artist holding the salt draining 'barrow' had been commissioned to produce a sculpture for the new underpass inspired by salt – it was vandalised within weeks of being unveiled.

Right: In 1973 the Archaeology Group was able to re-open a small Salt Museum in the library in preparation for a promised County Museum to be created in the former workhouse at Weaver Hall. The Committee Secretary (Lady Rochester) and the Hon. Curator (Brian Curzon) are shown putting the final touches to the display of old salt making tools.

Below: Railway lines to bring the limestone from Derbyshire had been important when choosing sites for the chemical works. Railway wagons loaded with chemicals can be seen outside Winnington Works. The works were built with numerous marshalling lines at the end of side lines. Throughout the '60s trade declined and many of the sidings were disused. In recent years the rail trade has become more popular as it is more economic for bulk transport, avoiding traffic and fuel taxes.

Works House or Platt Hall which stood at Lostock from 1660 had been used as a management dining room and then as an orders office, but expensive repairs made it unviable. In the middle of the works it was hardly a desirable residence and at the end of the twentieth century it was taken apart, the wood that could be saved was treated and it was rebuilt in the parkland at Bostock.

A familiar name vanished from the town in the 1990s. ICI, which absorbed Brunner Mond in 1926 decided to concentrate on medical chemicals. The heavy chemical works, including Lostock, were taken over by a new company using the old name of Brunner Mond and a new Salt Union took over the salt production. Once almost a company town for ICI, there are now no ICI job opportunities locally.

Restoration work started on the Anderton Lift in the 1990s, and the site was being landscaped when this photo was taken. It took a Lottery grant to pay for full restoration and to open a new information centre there. The first boat to pass through the restored lift did so in the Golden Jubilee year of 2003.

This late 1960s carnival parade emerges from the High Street through the Bull Ring to cross
the Town Bridge. In the background the gas tower, as ever, is the main feature. The bank stands
where the Angel Hotel (pictured elsewhere) had once stood. Many changes can be seen and in
the background the crane is above the nearly completed County Offices. An old double-decker
bus is amongst the traffic held up in Watling Street where the ancient salt works once were.

This comic band are marching into history in 1972. High Street would soon become a pedestrian way and Boots chemist was to move to a new building behind a preserved façade in Witton Street. The pavements are wet indicating rain, and so the spectators watch through the glass doors of the shops. Pedestrianisation made shopping less dangerous, but took away the old processional routes and replaced much old property with vast car parks.

Coomb's department store in Witton Street in the 1930s. In the window are the elegant and slinky long clothes of the time, when electricity to light shop window displays was a novelty. The plate glass 'tunnel entrance' and island display windows provide a contrast to what had gone before.

This picture of Woolworth's was taken forty years later when people were getting used to the novelty of a pedestrianised main street, with benches to sit under blossom trees in streets where the busy traffic once flowed. The town slowly emerged, saving as many timber buildings as possible to preserve the character of the place.

By the 1980s the paved way on 'Ship Hill' in Northwich had become a convenient shopping mall, attracting shoppers from many parts of the county with its wide range of shops and attractive timber buildings. It was named after the Ship Inn which stood where the centre shop is, and was once notorious for 'timber limbers': horse-drawn carts who would emerge from Leicester Street on the left before climbing the hill and vanishing into the timber yards in Timber Lane.

Christmas shoppers in the 1980s enjoy the fruits of so many years of redevelopment. The black and white shops were designed in the 1890s to withstand the subsidence to the pedestrian way of the 1970s. While the buildings in front are in the ancient township of Witton, when they cross a zebra crossing above the old 'cut' to the cotton mill they enter Northwich township.

Other local titles published by The History Press

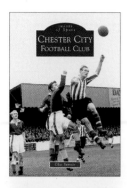

Chester City Football Club

CHAS SUMNER

Containing over 220 images, this book illustrates the history of Chester City and traces the progress of the club from its pre-League days, through its sixty-nine years of Football League membership, to the disastrous day when the club were relegated out of the league, in May 2000.

    Compiled by Chas Sumner, a supporter of more than thirty years and the club's official historian, this book is certain to revive memories for Chester supporters both past and present.

0 7524 2420 3

Cheshire Salt Country Then and Now

J. BRIAN CURZON

In this book, over 80 archive photographs have been carefully matched with photographs of the same scenes taken today. The old vistas include the cotton mills and smoking chimneys of the salt industry, the horse-drawn coach on its way to Northwich market and the salt barges on the River Weaver. The modern views offer an intriguing contrast between the street-corner pubs and rows of brick houses, with the department stores and congested roads which have replaced them.

0 7524 2675 3

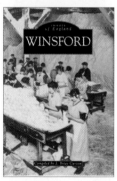

Winsford

J. BRIAN CURZON

This fascinating collection of over 200 photographs, many from a private archive, explores the town of Winsford from the 1880s to the 1980s.

    The creation of the town from the two areas on each side of the river, Over and Wharton, gives the area a fascinating and varied history. The town has been much developed in recent years, attracting new industries and business, and is a very different place from the days when chimneys from the salt works lined the banks of the river, their endless smoke helping to create the nickname of Dark Town.

0 7524 2774 X

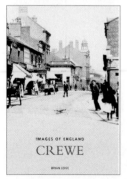

Crewe

BRIAN EDGE

Known as the town where people went to change trains, this recollection of Crewe and surrounding district captures the nostalgia of the years between 1895 and 1960, illustrating the changing face of the town during this time and the impact of the railway interchange.

    Drawing from amateur and professional collections of photographs and postcards, this volume will creates an evocative portrait of Crewe that will refresh many readers memories.

0 7524 3004 1

If you are interested in purchasing other books published by The History Press, or in case you have difficulty finding any of our books in your local bookshop, you can also place orders directly through our website

www.thehistorypress.co.uk